PRAY
In Your Own Voice
THROUGH WRITING

Virginia Phelan, Ph.D.

LIGUORI
PUBLICATIONS

One Liguori Drive
Liguori, MO 63057-9999
(314) 464-2500

> Dedication
> For three Graces:
> Sisters Bernarde, Maire, and Hiline

ISBN 0-89243-682-4
Library of Congress Catalog Card Number: 94-78949

Copyright © 1994, Virginia Burke Phelan
Printed in the United States of America
First Edition

All rights reserved. No part of this booklet may be reproduced, stored in a retrieval system, or transmitted without the written permission of Liguori Publications.

Cover design by Wendy Barnes

Contents

INTRODUCTION 5

Chapter One
WHY WRITE? 7

Chapter Two
RESISTING RESISTANCE 10

Chapter Three
JOURNALS 15

Chapter Four
LETTERS 24

Chapter Five
STORIES 34

Chapter Six
NEWSPAPER PIECES 43

Chapter Seven
LISTS 49

Chapter Eight
FILL IN THE BLANKS 56

APPENDIX
   TEN TIPS FOR PRAYING IN YOUR OWN VOICE 61
   FOR RETREAT DIRECTORS 61
   FOR FURTHER READING 63

INTRODUCTION

DON'T READ THIS BOOK

If you're looking for a book that describes prayer, this isn't it—at least not in the traditional sense. This book will help you to pray rather than to think about praying. It works well when you do, when you write as well as you read.

Nor is this a book only about writing. Writing is one goal here, but it's also a means, a way to journey prayerfully.

Instead, this guide helps you discover and develop your "voice" so you can pray as you are instead of as you think you should be. You don't need special training to do this because you already have what you need: your own words and experiences.

So please don't just read this book; *try* it as you read. If you do, you'll find out more about yourself. You'll also find that you're praying. And when you do, you'll discover that God is present when you are.

"PRAY ALWAYS?"

Does that seem impossible? When you're struggling to find a few minutes to yourself, do you wonder how anyone can follow Saint Paul's advice?

You're not alone. However, the difficulty may lie in the way we learned to think about prayer rather than with prayer itself. For example, I learned that prayer was different from life. Prayer happened in special places: beside dinner tables and beds. Really "good" prayer happened in church.

I also learned that prayer required special postures and special words. I felt I had to do it "right." Finally, I learned that prayer had to have a special, polite tone. The idea that God would listen to, even welcome my anger or impatience never occurred to me. God surely couldn't like my "bad" side.

Because of these notions, I formed some good habits and learned some beautiful prayers. But I was also bound by the habits that shaped me. If I didn't observe the "rules," I felt guilty. I saw God as the judgmental dispenser of hard-to-merit blessings. I tried to make deals to win God over. Most important, I didn't really enjoy praying and never guessed that I could.

Does this sound familiar?

When I finished school, worked, married, had children, worked some more, and went back to school, I continued to pray in the only way I knew. Fortunately, life's built-in hurdles kept stopping me. I became impatient with programmed prayer and angry with God because, even though I had done all the "right" things, my life was unsettled.

One day, I sat at the dining room table and wrote what I was thinking and feeling. I used my own words—angry words as hot as that August afternoon. When I was finished, I felt better.

I also felt God's presence. I started to discover that prayer really is a conversation between God and me and, to have that dialogue, I had to be there and speak in my own voice.

What voice is that? It's the one that is so much mine that it identifies me as me. I can't talk to God unless I use the voice God gave me, and that means using its full range: highs and lows, shouts and whispers.

That's all God asks. And God asks in that sometimes still, often small, voice inside us. God's voice can be heard in my own voice—and in yours.

Chapter One

WHY WRITE?

*I hear and I forget. I see and I remember.
I do and I understand.*

CHINESE PROVERB

If you regard writing as the rough equivalent of filling out your tax return, maybe you've never really learned to write. You may have dutifully, even enthusiastically, practiced your printed letters. Shortly after you mastered (or tried to master) cursive writing, however, you ran into "right" ways and "right" answers. You were luckier than most if, for a while, you were encouraged to write whatever you wanted, to simply tell your story.

I'm not suggesting that grammar doesn't matter. Too often, however, writing becomes merely a means of delivering a prescribed answer and the need for correctness extinguishes the instinctive, the spontaneous, even the truthful. It's as if neatness were the goal in thinking as well as in handwriting.

REWRITING DESCARTES

The elevation of the precisely rational is the legacy of René Descartes, the seventeenth-century French philosopher who rejected sensory evidence and accepted only the evidence of reason. His "I think; therefore, I am" has both guided and constrained Western consciousness, influencing societies (and thus schools) to trust what is linear, analytical, abstract, sequential, rational, and directed, and to distrust what is nonlinear, relational, concrete, concurrent, intuitive, and free.

This bias toward what psychologists call left-brain dominance has resulted in our learning that even a potentially freeing skill like writing ought to be controlled and correct in the "real" world where rewards are given. Imagine taking an exam and answering an essay question on the causes of the French Revolution by writing, "I don't care and I don't want to write about this, so I'll write about the butterfly I saw on the way to school."

Such writing (though it probably wouldn't earn a passing grade) not only shows a real understanding of revolution, it enables true questioning. Honest, thoughtful, precise writing *is* a way of thinking and of growing. Perhaps if Descartes had noticed that his hand was moving along with his brain, he would have penned "I write; therefore, I am" and avoided the excessive harnessing of both writing and thought in his wake.

Instead, the process of writing developed false distinctions. A few specially gifted but not always reliable types could do "creative" work, while almost everyone else used writing as a tool for transmitting information or managing people and ideas. Writing was a practical necessity, its practicality underlined by a suspicion of enjoyment that was another widespread legacy of the seventeenth century. Puritanism overshadowed inquisitiveness: writing was serious business, solemnly executed. No wonder we avoid it!

CHARTING THE TERRITORY

Yet writing can open frontiers if we let it. Just as early explorers took step after step and discovered undreamed-of lands and resources, so writing word by word helps us see our present and our possibilities. Accounts of where we've been and where we are show us options, so we choose with all the knowledge and understanding available at a given moment.

Writing is an aid to and a means of discernment. Mark Twain put it lightly when he commented that he didn't really know what he meant until he wrote it down. The process of mapping mental and spiritual topography with words requires attentiveness, energy, and often courage. But only by charting the terrain can we find the best—perhaps the only—true passage towards the undiscovered in ourselves.

GETTING THERE FROM HERE

If you've ever tried to read a map of unfamiliar territory, you know that the first thing you have to do after figuring out which way is north is to find where you are. Only then can you search for the most efficient or the most scenic way to proceed. As you reach your destination, you enlarge your perspective; you are no longer quite the same person you were when you started out.

Writing can help you grow even if you never pack a suitcase. For although the physical world has many more than seven wonders, your inner world holds inexhaustible curiosities, spectacles, and treasures. Your spiritual universe exceeds the physical one.

That's why Emily Dickinson didn't have to leave Amherst to see the sea and why small children, poets, and mystics don't need other people to fill up their time and their lives even if they do enjoy company. You can be your own companion too. And when you are, you will also be an invaluable fellow traveler.

But first you need to know where you are, to find your location on your own map. Writing will help you focus on "here" so you can get "there"—which is only "here" with a little writing in front of it.

Chapter Two

RESISTING RESISTANCE

*Nothing in life is to be feared;
it is only to be understood.*

MARIE CURIE

BEFRIENDING TIME

Even if you're convinced that writing will help you think clearly, see fully, and grow steadily, you might still believe that you can't make room for anything else in your daily schedule. You probably feel you're living out the old game show that challenged players to "name that tune" before the clock ran down.

The notion that clocks should be beaten, that time should be raced against, reflects our "hurry-itis." Clarence Day (*Life With Father*) seemed silly when he insisted on industrial efficiency at home. But we don't need someone standing by with a stopwatch to make us hustle; all we have to do is get up in the morning.

Imagine unwinding the clock, just taking out the spring and uncoiling it. Imagine slowing the ticking, changing the clock from a time bomb to a time balm. You can if you learn to treat time as an asset for use instead of a rack for stretching.

It's a two-step process. First you learn to turn time off by turning a timer on. Use a digital watch or an ordinary egg timer and set it for five, ten, or even better, twenty minutes. Then ignore it. This frees you because you know that just for now, you can work/write/play and at least start something. You also know that when the period is over, you'll be reminded (re-minded) about time. Then you can go on to another project, or you can continue doing the one you started.

That's why twenty minutes is an ideal segment: short enough to avoid fear of endless effort and physical discomfort, long enough to allow immersion. You can face spending twenty minutes on anything if you know there's a comfortable limit.

Of course, you can simply glance at a clock. But having to look up diverts your energy and disturbs your concentration so that it's hard to focus, which is the second step of befriending time. Focusing means reminding yourself that you're going to do what's in front of you. So if you're writing, you need only concern yourself with finding and using words. If you've never tried this, you may be surprised at how good you feel after simply focusing.

There's another way you can make time work for you instead of letting it drive or pressure you. You can choose to use it for yourself first. Financial experts insist that the only way to make money serve you is to pay yourself first, *before* you pay your bills. You have a chronological economy, too, and it only thrives when you put a little time aside for yourself (early in the day if possible) before you exhaust your supply.

When you give yourself time before your "real work," you send a powerful message to your *self*: "I matter too." Not surprisingly, your self responds positively, and the interest on this investment shows up as energy, insight, and awareness.

But first you have to start, however briefly. You need to take time, instead of letting time overtake you.

BLANK PAGE PANIC

You've set a timer or set aside a few minutes and are ready to write. Now what? Ideally, you have something you want to record and can start there. It could be a word that stayed with you from something you read or a conversation you had. It could be a feeling or a question or a hope. It could be a dream fragment.

But if you're like most of us, you see all that open space and panic. "What can I write?" you think. That question really means, "What can I write that's *right*?" At the start of any project, our wonderful, helpful left brains often take over, and we begin to judge ourselves. Other people are writers, we think, but we're certainly not. In fact, we're wasting time. We'd better do something useful.

We're wise to view the start of any enterprise with caution, as Japanese brush painters do the blank page. They know that the first stroke establishes the direction of the whole piece, so that first stroke matters.

It matters for us, too, but it matters because we're beginning, not because we have to have a beautiful or even presentable end. It matters because we're choosing to search as we search for words. It matters because we can start a dialogue with our real selves.

Still—we're stuck. We might as well stop this foolishness, we think. But when we're stuck, we're not being foolish enough. We need to get the better of words—with words.

WORDS WITHOUT END

Hamlet read them. Eliza Doolittle hated them. Politicians inflate them. Poets master them. And we command lots of them—except when we want to.

How can we tame them? By not taking them too seriously. Try these suggestions:

- Start with any word, followed by any other: rhymes, alliterations, made-up words, names. If you can't think of anything, write the same word repeatedly. Remember: you're just writing words, and they can always be changed. You don't need to know where they're going; just receive them and record them.
- Run words together in impossible sequences to make new ones.
- Write as fast as you can.
- Keep your pencil (or pen) and hand in contact with the page.
- Record *everything*, even if it seems silly. Ignore your internal critic.

The basic principle here is "Move the hand, move the brain." We know that signals pass from the hand through the synapses and up the arm until they reach the spinal cord and the brain. So moving the hand sends messages to the brain, even if it takes a short while to get them through. (You might also want to try a special application of just writing words by looking at Chapter Seven, "Lists.")

CHILD'S PLAY AND OTHER STRATEGIES

Because being stuck most often comes from fear of not measuring up to our left brain's judgments, we need to get around its strictures and let our right brains out to play. It's as if we said to our left brains, "I value your help, and I'll have plenty for you to do later. But right now I'm just playing. Relax. I'll call you."

Writing, discovering ideas, and exploring ourselves is truly play. Unlike games with scores, this play is open-ended, an invitation to our spirits and ourselves. It is, therefore, a path to and a part of prayer.

So starting and restarting to write thrives on playful strategies for getting unstuck. The first of these involves seeing the page not as an object to be filled but as a space for adventure.

Imagine the page as a clear sidewalk on a day at the very start of summer vacation. You can make signs or write greetings or outline a hopscotch box.

Or imagine the page as a wall just stripped of paper, awaiting its new covering. You can write messages to the future or draw scenes from the past and know they'll be there even when you've moved on.

Or imagine the page as a yard full of new snow, inviting you to come and make angels or snow figures or igloos or ice palaces. You can make any shape you want, as long as you go outside (inside) and surround yourself with whiteness.

Other playful ploys can free you and get you going. Experiment with your own or try these:

- Write the longest word in the world.
- Write from the center outward or from the perimeter inward.
- Write from the bottom to the top of the page.
- Write from right to left.
- Scribble.
- Doodle or draw.
- Write in color. Match your feeling.

All of these (and any others you invent) build on the move-the-hand, move-the-brain principle. So keep moving, even if—especially if—you feel silly. Being silly is better than being stuck and will probably thaw your mental freeze.

THE NIKE SOLUTION

You've undoubtedly heard that when faced with anything intimidating, you should just do it. This theory assumes that starting will get you past your stage fright and settle your fluttering stomach. If you remember the times when your pre-event nervousness dissipated as you progressed, you can remind yourself that you've felt uneasy before and it will pass.

So start writing what you're feeling. You can say, "I really don't want to do this today—or any day. I hate writing, even if it's supposed to help me. I hate it."

But don't stop there. Add "because" to "I hate it," and finish the sentence. Then, recall a time when you hated writing. In doing this, you will reclaim a piece of yourself, learn about what made you fearful, and understand how you got to where you are a little better. You won't have instant clarity, but you'll have more light and less shadow. And where there's more *you*, there's more growth and more prayer.

The conversation that is prayer needs two voices: God's and yours. Simply getting on with writing who and what you are can help you find your voice.

JUST SAY "NO"

If you can't bring yourself to face the page on a particular day, don't. Decide that you won't write that day *and begin to do something else*. Note that you don't just lie in bed or swing in a hammock (though those are fine things to do too). You begin your day determined that you won't write—you won't even try.

What usually happens is—you guessed it—you become aware of something you really need to say. Often this occurs soon after you start a routine task, partly from the freeing effect of not pushing and partly from engaging in the familiar. Repetition lets the mind get out of overdrive. When the mind isn't straining, it happily produces ideas and questions and connections.

That's why blankness often responds to repeated physical activity. Walking, swimming, and running all make initial demands, but once you're in a "groove," you're free to gather wool or daisies. Your biggest problem then may be to catch and hold on to what surfaces in you while you are otherwise occupied.

So if you're really stuck, don't write. Get up and move briskly. Put index cards in your pocket and head for the sidewalk, the road, the garden—any place you can get physical. Immerse yourself in that other activity and focus on it. Your spirit will meet you there, and your voice will be close behind.

Chapter Three

JOURNALS

Existence is like many rivers flowing to one sea.

LAO TZU

Have you ever listened to yourself on a recording and been surprised by the way you sound? "That's not me," I thought the first time I heard myself on tape. "That sounds like my sister." We have trouble hearing ourselves accurately because our ears hear our own voices differently from the way they hear other sounds. We get modifications from physical structures, vibrations, breathing, and stress. We hear all this from two exterior sides, with the voice projecting out front and from the inside too. No wonder we don't know how we sound.

If we need practice in hearing the outer, physical voice, we also need practice in hearing the inner voice. This is the voice that speaks the real person, the one behind the masks, under the layers, in the depths of the soul. This is the voice of the true self, the voice we want for prayer.

It is also the voice of the prayer dialogue we were born for, for God speaks clearly, but God's voice gets buried by "important" noise. The story of Elijah in 1 Kings 19:9, 11-13 gives us a clue. Elijah went to a cave and was told to go out and stand before Yahweh. The prophet saw a hurricane, but Yahweh wasn't in it. Neither was Yahweh in the earthquake that followed nor the fire that came next. Then Elijah heard "a sound of sheer silence," and he knew it as a sign of the Presence.

Elijah couldn't hear Yahweh at all until he withdrew to that cave. While most of us can't hide physically as he did, we can seek the shelter of solitude right where we are, in our ordinary lives. All we need to do is start journaling.

THE WRITTEN JOURNAL

When you think of a journal, you probably picture a book. You might know about personal journals like Thomas Merton's or fictional journals like Daniel Defoe's *A Journal of the Plague Year* or journals of medical research like *The Lancet*. Journals are for professionals but not for you, right?

Wrong. Journals are definitely for you and for all those who want to live their journeys, not just drift on them. Journals record where we've been, suggest where we're headed, and help us find our paths.

WHAT'S THE DIFFERENCE?

A journal is a record of a search. Like any record, it refers to events. Unlike a diary, however, it doesn't aim to record what you wore to the office Christmas party. In addition, unlike most written records, a journal makes feelings as important as facts. Feelings *are* facts, after all; they're in us whether we acknowledge them or not.

A journal not only notes feelings, it also traces them. Faithfully kept entries can pinpoint when an emotional climate begins to change, even if the change is subtle and can only be detected in retrospect. That's why dating entries helps.

My journal, for example, chronicles a particularly dark time when, through no fault of my own, I was unable to do what I love: teach. I wrote every day, sometimes several times a day, about how I felt. The writing couldn't fix anything outside me, but it did help me fix on my anger (with my employer, my chairman, God), my sadness, and my grief. In recording my feelings, I became clear about where I was, what I could control (not much!), and what I had to accept. The act of writing helped me to find and feel peace.

But a journal not only records emotions; it also notes—and therefore, helps to develop—ideas. The same entries that show my shadowed months also show my growing awareness that I could do more than teach, or teach differently. The many-sided work I do today grew directly from my increasingly clear notions that I could use my public voice in ways I never would have tried if I had continued along the old, safe path. This book is one outgrowth of that period.

If there is a prescription for a journal, it's this: don't look for prescriptions. By its nature, a journal is open-ended and exploratory. There is never enough time to complete one, and there is never so little time that you can't start one.

Because it has no specific subject, anything goes in a journal. You can react to an event, record new information, or reflect on a reading. You can respond to an art form or begin to shape one; prose can shift to poetry or give way to pictures.

Keeping a journal says "I'm worth it" to yourself, and that helps you claim you own power. Since, like so many people, you may feel increasingly powerless, journaling writes in a vote for yourself. When you decide to listen to your own voice, you feel more able to cope with others.

Journaling is also a way to find and increase the yield on your resources. Even if you never plan to write anything else, you find many points for consideration, meditation, or consultation.

And that's the best reason of all for keeping a journal: discovery. You discover yourself in the clear mirror you create when you write from your core. You notice what's real, and by noticing it, you grow. You let what's shadowed come to light and claim all of the you that's already there.

You also discover your voice and find you have something to say. No tentative "Well, I think..." and other verbal dodges here; you say who you are and what you see. When you do that, you're ready to listen for the "sound of sheer silence" that forms the other part of your prayer dialogue. You practice speaking from your spirit to the Spirit that lives and breathes, and if you stay still and listen, God speaks back.

WHAT TO USE

The short answer is: anything. It's almost that simple, but not quite.

When I began to journal as an adult, I used a pencil and loose-leaf paper because I had them. I moved to notebooks, the old marble-patterned ones and the less school-like pale green ones, and I wrote in ink when I had it, ballpoint when I didn't. I used several spiral-bound notebooks after having to keep a journal as part of a course. I also used hardbound books that friends and family gave me.

Then I used a typewriter, first a small manual one and then a racy, electric model. I was never as comfortable with these as I was with pencil and pen because I'm not a great typist and I had to correct so much. But after I realized I could just keep going, I wrote more freely and even began to enjoy the typos.

The low-tech phase ended when I bought a computer to do my "real" work. Once I learned word processing, I began to journal on screen. Strangely, using this seemingly uncreative machinery helped my searching while it helped my typing. Because I could retrieve and revise, I could go full speed, and my fingers began to fall where they belonged. The freedom to move around really helped.

There are advantages to all these materials. You might consider some of the following points:

- Journals are private, so choose accordingly. If you need to lock yours in a drawer, smaller is better.
- Loose pages allow rearrangement, but they also require containment. You don't want entries scattered around unless you live alone. Even then, your writing deserves the care you give your other treasures.
- If hardbound books intimidate you into thinking your entries have to be perfect, use ordinary notebooks. Unlined paper allows you to do little drawings, should you want to, but lines make writing easier for most people.
- Remember: move the hand, move the brain. Writing by hand produces more movement than typing, so it might help you start. When I want to think about something that's elusive, I often use a "No. 2" pencil. The movement of the graphite on paper feeds back to my brain and nudges it.
- Feel free to switch materials. I still take a seven-by-nine-inch notebook on trips. When I forget it, I use any available paper and add it to my notebook when I get home. I also vary paper and ink color. Have you ever written with a *real* purple pen?

CHALLENGING DISABILITIES

If you have limited use of your hands, you can use a personal computer and a program designed to provide assistance while allowing independence. One of these programs has an on-screen keyboard that responds to touch and reduces keystrokes. Using artificial intelligence, the package predicts and completes a writer's words, adapting that person's style. It also capitalizes and spaces automatically.

If you use a wheelchair, investigate a laptop or notebook computer. Programs that eliminate the need to use a keyboard or a mouse in conventional ways make these small machines respond to a range of pressures from heavy to light; keyboard overlays guide you. You can also get a program with a speech option to check your keystroke accuracy.

So if you have a learning disability, a language deficiency, or a physical restriction, you can write on a computer. But even if you can't use a conventional keyboard at all, you can still "type" with a head pointer or with a device that lets you turn and puff instead of pointing and clicking.

And this is only the current generation of programs! Soon you'll be able to speak into a computer and watch your words appear. Meanwhile, all the major computer companies have departments for special needs. They are eager to help, so ask them.

HOW TO FIND TIME

You've chosen your materials and want to start, but you think about your day and wonder when you can manage it. Even if you treat time as an ally and free yourself by using a timer, you can't see how to stretch your already overscheduled day. What good does setting a timer do if you can't find ten or twenty waking minutes?

Theoretically, you can journal at any time during the day. Practically, however, there are two good times, one better than the other. You can write early or late.

If you decide to write at night, you'll usually find it easy to start. Your feelings may be strong, making words come out faster than your hand can move. You can round off the day before sleep.

But letting your journal wait until the end of the day often means you don't get to it at all. Trains have delays, children get sick, relatives need help. Life intrudes and you get too tired, even though writing can help you settle your insides for the night.

So the better choice is to write early. I discovered that if I set the alarm a bit earlier than I absolutely have to get up, I can write first and then go on with the day. Since I'm not a morning person by temperament or constitution, it isn't always easy to roll out when the alarm sounds, but it's been worth the effort.

I stumble in to the computer, turn it on, and write. (The first week I did this I hit mostly wrong keys!) Except for the obvious disadvantage of having to awaken early, the gains have been enormous. By writing myself awake, I've been able to catch those fleeting, fragile ideas and images that live at the fringes of the dreamworld. I've also been able to connect with dreams that I otherwise would have lost.

In addition, the early hour lends itself to simple honesty and directness. I don't "overthink" things; I just say them. I also don't lose thoughts to the telephone or other people's needs. My only job during this time is to be me and say what's true.

So if you've never taken advantage of your early morning self, try the following:

- Set your alarm early for at least one week.
- Get up *as soon as* the alarm sounds. Groans are fine; just don't lie there or hit the "snooze button."
- Have your materials ready—beside the bed, if possible. If you use a computer, have your disk formatted, labeled, and named.
- Begin writing before you speak to anyone so you won't lose the whispers.
- Listen to what's inside and write it, no matter how silly it seems.

Whatever time you choose, *choose* it: think about it and schedule it. If you do, you'll be more likely to take it. We make time for what's important. *You're* important.

WHERE TO BEGIN

If you try early morning journaling, you'll probably focus on yourself, even if it's only to complain about having to get up. But if you're as blank as the page or the computer screen, or if you're writing late and you're too tired to think, you can try these suggestions:

- Start with the date. Add ideas that the date suggests. For example, I often measure the year by noting relationships to Christmas. So on June 24, I might write, "Six months till Christmas Eve." I also note birthdays and keep people in mind early in the day. Recording dates helps pinpoint developments and gets your hand—and your brain—going.
- Write about whatever sounds you hear, including sounds within yourself. I almost always wake to music, not on the radio but inside me. The music varies from childhood songs to symphonies to Fred Astaire tunes to pop. So if it's there, I name it and try to write down any words that might be part of it, since I often get direction or confirmation from them. Even if you don't hear music, you hear many sounds. At this moment, I hear the computer's hum, a distant plane, and several birds. If you write

what you hear, you're writing. Other ideas, like the associations you have with various sounds, will likely appear.
- Write about a dream or dream fragment. Do this early in the day, since fragile bits evaporate with consciousness. Sometimes they surface later; make notes if they do and write them out as soon as you can. Dreams form your own special symbolic language and offer rich possibilities.
- Write about an outstanding event and, more important, your feelings about it. Write to understand it and put it to rest. When an event has major consequences, writing both early and late allows you to recognize, accept, and integrate those effects more quickly than if you just stew and suffer.
- Complain. Write about how this is inconvenient and tiring and tedious. If you can only manage to grumble for days, you might find you have more to say. You might even start to laugh about it.

Remember, the biggest enemies of freedom in writing are the need to be correct and the desire to be clever. You're not trying to win the Nobel Prize; you're trying to grow into greater wholeness. And wholeness, as Merton observed, is holiness.

HOW MUCH IS ENOUGH?

If you've ever looked at published journals, you might have the impression that the writers thoroughly discussed all the issues they raised. But if you look again, you'll see that many passages are fragmentary. In Dag Hammarskjöld's *Markings*, for example, some ideas appear only as questions that don't get attention for months. Some never reappear.

So "real" journal entries consist of a word, a phrase, a sentence, a paragraph, a page, or any combination of these. Even if you have hours to spend on your journal, you need write only what you're moved to say. A short entry, genuinely felt, is much more authentic than pages of blah, blah, blah. Don't hide out, but don't drag on, either.

FOUR GUIDELINES

There are no rules for journaling. There are, however, guidelines that will help you develop your voice as you write. They'll help to develop your spoken voice, too, since as you become clearer about who you are, you'll be more able to project that.

As you write, remember:

1. Be open. Tune in to what's really happening in you. At first, you might have trouble figuring out what that is because our deepest concerns are often buried or masked. Listen for whispers; know you're encouraging your whole self. Thoughts matter but feelings matter more. There are no "shoulds" or "should nots" in journaling; *everything* is appropriate.
2. Be honest. Use words you really want to use, even if you hesitate to use them in your everyday speech. If you're angry, be *angry*! If you're disappointed, say so. If you're delighted, use words that might sound silly on the job. Make up words. Remember: there is no code of etiquette here.
3. Be faithful. When you decide to journal, you're making a promise to yourself. Keep it by writing regularly, daily, if possible. Schedule your journaling as you would anything else, and stick with it. The more faithful you are to your journal, the more you'll develop your voice and grow in prayer.
4. Be respectful. Honor your thoughts and feelings by valuing them. Realize that your efforts to grow show courage, even if you don't feel courageous. Foster timid beginnings and you will honor your spirit and your journey. God gave you all you need; let your journey—and yourself—unfold.

THE TAPED JOURNAL

Even if you find it difficult or impossible to write in the usual sense because of disability or dislocation, you can still "write" by using a tape recorder. Most of the suggestions for the written journal will also work for taping, but you'll want to modify some of them.

First, however, remember that you'll be using your voice in two ways: literally, as you speak, and metaphorically, as you express your true self. If you recall that Scripture sometimes shows God speaking to humans in ordinary, audible words, you'll know you're in good company when you write with sound. You might even find you have advantages, since you can add color and emphasis with tone. When you feel like singing, do; when you're angry, yell.

Getting past the blank may be more difficult for you than for others, since you aren't moving your hand. But you *are* moving your mouth and that counts. You might feel foolish as you begin, but if you're prepared for pauses, they won't keep you speechless long. Try using the questions at the end of this section if you get stuck.

Before you begin, however, you need to make three decisions:

- Choose your tape recorder. You'll find various models and degrees of sophistication. You don't need the most expensive machine, but if you have trouble using your hands, you'll want one that is voice-activated. It starts recording when you start talking and shuts down when you stop.
- Choose "normal" or "all-purpose" tapes. You don't need expensive, high-performance types. Find a safe storage place; a shoe box will hold about two dozen tapes if you stand them on end.
- Choose a place where you can talk freely. You want to speak openly about your awarenesses and feelings, and having to edit them will hinder you.

You'll also profit from having an ally who will help you with the mechanics of handling and storing tapes, and who will respect and support your search.

To help yourself start, try the following questions. If they don't strike a chord in you, however, ignore them. To use them most effectively, read them aloud and then keep going with your observations, reactions, and reflections. You can also use the questions in Chapter Eight, "Fill in the Blanks."

- I am happiest when…
- My best moment this week was…
- My greatest concern is…
- My greatest strength is…
- I wish I could have a conversation with…
- The person I think of as my model is…
- If I had a coat of arms, it would have…
- I sometimes wonder about…
- If I were a song, I'd be…
- If I could give one gift to the world, I'd give…

You have a special kind of courage and a unique voice. Let both help you grow and pray.

Chapter Four

LETTERS

*But all shall be well, and all shall be well,
and all manner of thing shall be well.*

JULIAN OF NORWICH

When I want to jumpstart a project, I often write a letter. It helps me get my brain going, of course, but it also keeps me present. I can't write a letter from the distant "out there." I can only write it from "in here," in my own voice.

Letters also help me pray. I discovered this one evening when I was restless and couldn't settle into "real" prayer. I didn't know what to do, but I did know that letter writing made me focus. So I sat down and started to type "Dear God." When I finished, I felt better. Writing that letter gave me peace. It also made me laugh.

Letters can help you, too, especially when you're stuck. But if the only letters you ever read begin "Dear Cardholder," you're probably wondering how they can help you pray in your own voice. They can't if you write in the distant "it seems" mode. If you invest yourself, however, you'll start to see your subject and yourself clearly and then you can grow. In fact, writing letters might be the best way to develop your voice.

Letters work because they're always written to a "you." Even bulk-mail letters are directed to a specific audience. This appeal to a "you" makes you choose the most precise words you can find to clarify yourself to your "reader." If you've ever had to do a cover letter for a resume, you know how important it is to choose your words wisely.

Letters also assume a distance, physical or emotional. They can be both the bridges you build and the vehicles you use to cross from your "side" to the other person's. At the national and personal levels, they can make—or destroy—peace.

Personal letters live. Because they can be confidential, even intimate, they develop your voice in ways that journals can't. Although the most reflective journals become notes to the self, they don't *have* to be addressed to anyone. Letters do because they form half of a dialogue.

Just as you can't have even a brief spoken conversation without revealing something about yourself and your view of the other person, letters "speak" for and about you. That's why we're fascinated by other people's correspondence. A famous general's letters, a president's notes, a suicide's parting words—these give us windows into real souls. Novelists sometimes tell whole tales through letters.

Letters make us keep our audience clearly present as we write. Although we address the other person, we also talk to ourselves, receiving insights while spelling out our views. We're always aware of the other person, but we have to focus on our own words. Marriage Encounter and other self-help groups know this and use letter writing to strengthen ties.

As a letter writer, you must keep your partner in mind as you write about an issue. At the same time, you can concentrate on your side of it without being distracted by facial expressions or interrupted before you can finish your sentence. And when you exchange letters, the reading process allows the same mindful, complete attention.

So letters work. They also bring joy through the writing, even about painful issues, since they absorb and transport. As you may have discovered in journaling, real joy comes from being as engaged as humans can be. Or to paraphrase Saint Paul, "complete presence casts out pain."

You can pray through letters in three ways: by writing to yourself, to others, and to God. All are love letters. Here are some ideas to get you started. As with the suggestions for journaling, feel free to adapt them.

LETTERS TO YOURSELF

Do you ever talk to yourself? Writing to yourself, because it's more conscious than talking to yourself, helps you understand how you got to wherever you are. Once you see that, you can be more patient and understanding with yourself and with others too.

For example, try writing to yourself as a child. Your present adult self addresses your former—but still present—child self about a difficulty or feeling. You focus on *today* as an outgrowth of your history. If you didn't "unpack" your emotional baggage then, you can "unpack" it now.

Before you start, however, consider your materials. Although you can use the same ones you used for your journal, you might want to change. For example, you'll get a truer sense of writing to your still present child if you use real letter paper. Think about color and choose one that comforts you. Your goal is to reassure the hurting little person inside, so use anything that makes you feel safe. Here are some guidelines for the content of the letter:

- Begin with "Dear _____," using your childhood name. If you disliked that name, use the one you preferred. (One person called me "Frog Eyes" and it stuck, even though I don't have eyes like a frog and didn't like the name.) If your childhood and adult names are the same, consider addressing your earlier self as "Dear little _____," unless that feels too awkward.
- Continue with something like "I know you're upset about _____." Be specific. As I write this now, I know I still don't like being called unattractive or unfair names, so I would write about that.
- Comfort the child in you. For example, you might assure her that you understand her pain and know how being hurt can make her want to hurt back. You could write about how pain seems to take over completely so the whole body hurts. Say what your heart suggests. If you keep that small child in mind (an old picture helps), you'll find the words.
- Now tell the child what your adult self will do to make it better. Assurances such as "I'll protect you now" or "You're not alone now" are possibilities. Write what you needed to hear.
- Close the letter with "Love" and sign it as "Big _____" if that feels right. Notice how you feel as you're writing (loving? protective?) and when you're finished (relieved? comforted?). Reflect quietly. If you have time, let your younger self write back. Use materials the child in you would like. Whatever happened to that pencil box and those crayons? Try them now.

This way of addressing a memory helps heal it. And because you're present, even while dealing with the past, it's also a kind of prayer.

LETTERS TO OTHERS

In one sense, even a letter to yourself is a letter to another because you are no longer the same person you were. But this section shows you some of the ways that writing to real "other" people helps you strengthen your voice and grow in prayer too.

There are so many possibilities that you can spend the rest of your life sampling them. To start, try these

- "I've wanted to tell you..."

Write to a living friend, spouse, teacher, or employer. Tell that person something you haven't yet been able to say. This could be about a dream or goal you have, a concern (for yourself or the other person), or a secret you've been unable to share. It could also express your thanks. When you finish the letter, consider sending it.

- "To be opened in the event of my death."

Address your survivors, telling them things they need or have a right to know that you've been unwilling or unable to reveal. Be as detailed as you can since your letter may be the only guidance they have on the subject. If they need to locate something, give directions, draw a map, and specify exactly what they should look for. Put the completed letter wherever you store important papers.

Survivors also need to know your wishes about your final days (one letter) and funeral arrangements (a second letter). Perhaps you have trouble talking about those things (or they might have trouble hearing it). Remember that by making such decisions yourself and conveying them, you are showing your love. You are relieving already troubled people of the painful burden of making choices. Store these letters safely too.

Writing to the living keeps you mindful of them and lets you hold them closely but openhandedly. You embrace, but your arms aren't locked. Julian of Norwich wrote that God surrounds us like clothing, encompassing but not smothering us. Letters to the living fill us with life and give life to others at the same time.

- "I never told you..."

Write to a deceased parent or relative. Tell that person something you were unable to discuss when he or she was living. Maybe you couldn't talk about it; maybe the other person couldn't hear it. Writing about a memory will help you heal, just as writing to your childhood self does. After you finish the letter and reflect, write the deceased person's reply. You might be surprised at what you find yourself saying.

You can also write about what you know you learned from or owe to that person. This recognition not only allows you to note your own abilities or gifts, it also reminds you that immortality isn't merely an abstract concept. People live on through such legacies to others. I find great comfort, for example, in seeing how my parents live in and through me.

- "I've wanted to ask you…"

This can also begin a letter to a deceased person. Ask the person about a piece of your history that needs clarifying. You might want facts, but you might also want to know what he or she would say about a troubling situation you're in now. Framing your question explicitly helps you retrieve lost bits from your own memory so that when you write your "answer," you can use the other person's perspective.

- "Why didn't you tell me…?"

If you've made a discovery you wish you had known about earlier, perhaps you're angry about what was withheld. You need to honor that feeling. Don't leave it there, though. Write the response. Then notice how you feel toward the person who withheld the information and write a few words about that feeling. Remember, these letters are not about blaming but about healing. Healing helps wholeness, which helps prayer.

- "We've Never Met…"

Imagine yourself at the age of eighty writing to a young person about what you now believe. This person could be an actual relative or other youth in your present circle, or you could address a descendent. Does your view of "history" shift when you think about those who will look back to—and maybe want to ask questions of—you?

Write as specifically as you can. My own letter, if I wrote it today, would reflect many of my current choices but include others. For instance, I would spend more time with a special friend I miss. I would go to the White Mountains of New Hampshire more often. I would take a hot-air balloon ride. And I would eat more cookies.

This shows me what I could add to my life now to make it more nourishing. Writing it down makes it clearer for me, and it will for you too. But writing this letter also tests and reinforces principles I've tried to live by. I might tell my young reader to heed the wise person who observed that no one on a deathbed ever wished she had spent more time at the office. I would also urge seeking work that feeds the spirit as well as the body. And I would insist that "faith" has many pathways—including finding one's true voice through writing!

If I wrote my letter tomorrow, it might be slightly different, but it would still be explicit about where I want to go. This exercise reminds me, should I ever forget, that older people are resources I'd be foolish to ignore and that I'm inexorably heading toward old age myself.

LETTERS TO GOD

Writing letters to God shrinks the distance you sometimes feel when you try to pray. Addressing God as "you" forces you to leave abstractions to the theorists. In this exchange, there are only "I" and "you." And exchange it is. But first, there has to be an "I," with all the feelings and language of that "I." If those elements are missing, there's no dialogue.

God wants this exchange so much that when Moses asked how to name the one who sent him with the Commandments, God replied, "I AM." The God of the Bible is a person, so God is the model for the whole "I" you want to become.

Letters not only help you develop your voice as you develop your "I," they also help you expand your view of what God cares about. In this exchange, you sense that if you care about the silly, especially if you *see* it as silly, God cares about that as much as about the serious.

As a result, you become less likely to reserve prayer for "important" or "proper" times and places. You find yourself beginning to pray—that is, to connect in your exchange—more often. You begin to suspect that continual prayer is possible because there's no subject unworthy of it, no heartfelt language that's inappropriate.

If this frightens you, you're not alone. I used to be reluctant to open up to God too. For example, I was angry, whether I said so or not, but I never thought using angry words with God could be prayerful. Then one day when I couldn't settle into "nice" prayer, I followed my feeling and wrote God a letter. When I finished, I had a real sense of God's presence and care. God listened to me because I listened to myself, my childish, angry, hurt self.

God listens to your "I," whatever emotional coloring you're wearing. So try writing to God. You may get a response you never expected.

Your letters to God don't have to be angry. They can start from whatever fills you or holds you back. Notice that they "start from...." If you write to a friend, you might have a direction but you don't have an outline. Even if you occasionally note several points you want to make, most of the time you probably just begin and let one thing suggest another. Anything you forget ends up in a "P.S."

When you write to God, do the same thing. Start where you are and let the details come. As with all your writing, be specific. Begin with what you're feeling and why. "God, I'm sad today because..." God may already know it, but you might not have figured out why you're sad, and even if you do know, you gain by spelling it out.

Close with what feels right. If you're angry, you won't want to close with "Love." Say, "Impatiently" or whatever it is you're feeling, then sign your name. This might feel silly. But you're writing a letter, and signing it gives it *your* mark, which is part of your identity.

Some of your subjects could include:

Fear. Mel Brooks says that everything in the world happened because of fear: inventions, institutions, laws—everything. Anthony De Mello says that fear is one of the two emotions we have (the other is love). Whether you agree or not, you feel fear at least some of the time. When you do, write about it. Describe your physical symptoms (stomach tension? headache?). Specify when the fear feels most threatening (at three a.m.? when you have to ask for something from a boss?).

Detail your situation just as you would to an attentive, nonjudgmental friend. Ask for help or ask a question or ask for a specific result.

Gratitude. Brother David Steindl-Rast says that gratefulness is the heart of prayer. Gratitude makes us remember that we're creatures who benefit from the Love that can only give. And because we recognize that we've received, we also want to give, making us co-creators with God.

So when you're thankful, tell God why. Remember your childhood school exercise and list the people and things you feel grateful for. Let your words be fruits of your spirit; you don't need many, but they can be as rich and colorful as the rainbow of treasures each of us has received.

Need. This is the only kind of prayer some of us consistently practiced for whole periods of our lives. Then when we grew "sophisticated," we shrank from the idea of appearing childish, always asking, begging, pleading. We thought it was mere whining. But petitionary prayer is sound prayer; in fact, it's necessary and healthy.

We need help and we need to acknowledge that we need help. Modern twelve-step programs grow from the notion that before we can start to recover, we have to admit we have difficulties we can't handle, and we have to ask for help.

So God doesn't need to hear your requests, but you need to make them. Otherwise, you might be tempted to think you're in charge. By making requests, you begin to clarify just what you can do and what you can't. You also move your requests to the front of your awareness, where you'll be more likely to help yourself by cooperating with grace.

Asking also teaches patience and persistence. The widow in Scripture who kept insisting (Luke 18) and the three-year-old inside you that tugged at adult hands share the same healthy energy. You *have* to ask clearly, specifically, faithfully. And then you have to ask again. Writing helps you ask at least twice, physically and spiritually. It is this persistence that is rewarded

Discouragement. Discouragement means loss of heart, which may be the most common feeling in the Western world. Because we've learned that we must be productive to be valuable, when we can't achieve and earn in externally recognizable ways, we feel useless.

We have good reason to feel that way. We've been conditioned to define ourselves by our occupations. Yet we can't plan and control our life's work because jobs often disappear. Do you know someone whose career has vanished? Has yours?

We also define courage in grand, external ways—the Dirty Harry model. But Dag Hammarskjöld wrote that not running away from a difficulty is courageous. Do you think of courage that way? Are you running or standing?

Whatever you're doing, instead of blaming yourself, write to God about the job interview, the unanswered call, the rejected proposal. Use all the words you feel right now; then look at what you've written. Consider how you might feel toward someone who has just written the same thing to you. Reflect on what you might say.

Frustration. Frustration combines fear and discouragement with time pressure to produce a special kind of anger. The Latin root means "in vain," which could be seared on the forehead of anyone who's tried and tried—and failed. Have you felt frustration's heat in the past week?

Does repeated failure make you feel like a three-year-old unable to master the zipper? Do you feel you *are* frustrated, that it takes you over? Do you feel a trace of embarrassment when it does and hope that no one can see how your insides look?

Write about your efforts, expectations, and effects—or lack of them. Try to connect with an incident from your childhood or adolescence. Use the journalist's questions (who? what? where? when? why? how?) to help yourself recall the details. Specify sound, smell, color as they were when your outrage was hot. Those elements are still in you, so recreate the situation and they might surface.

Then link that incident with the current one. Tell God how this makes you feel: powerless, foolish, silly. Say what you think should have happened. Write boldly. If you normally write on a word processor, try writing by hand to allow variations and flourishes.

When you're finished, read over what you've said. If you can make it stronger, do so. Your purpose is not just to tell a story or make a complaint but to find voice for what usually chokes you. So raise the pitch of your written voice; then listen.

LETTERS FROM GOD

If you write one or more of the letters described above, you've exercised your voice and completed one half of the prayerful dialogue. To find the other part, you have to listen—but not to what's out there.

Prayer would be a lot easier if we could get an answering memo. But God doesn't usually give the twentieth-century equivalent of stone tablets. Instead, God speaks to us through what Elijah heard as that "sound of sheer silence" or, as some translations call it, a "still, small voice." To hear that voice, we have to go back into our own caves.

So after you use your voice, you use your ears. These are internal ears that receive messages through your imagination, instincts, and impulses. (Impulses often get bad press because some people let them take over and run everything, but you know that you've often had an impulse that has prompted you to kindness or generosity or forgiveness.) When you let them work, you let God speak.

Your method is the same: writing letters. But this time, before you write, do what God does: listen to yourself.

- Let your letter to God "cool" a little. Do something else, especially something physical. If you've written with your heart, you probably feel more peaceful than you did. If you're still agitated, walk away, even for a few minutes.
- Reread your letter slowly without making judgments. Your goal is not to think but to hear with feeling. If you're surprised by the intensity of what you've written, let your inner eyes widen, but read on. Remember, you're reading as God reads: eagerly, but patiently. Let the you of the letter reveal the real you.
- Respect what you "hear." The way you've described things in your letter is the way they look to you. God takes you seriously.
- Write back. Begin as you began before, with "Dear _____." Then say how you feel, responding to fear or gratitude or pain.
- Close as you feel moved to do, with "I'm waiting with you" or "I'm glad you told me" or simply "Love." Anything that fits is fine. Then sign it in some appropriate way.

If you use letters to give yourself a voice, you'll grow inevitably toward God. Like the sunflower that follows the light, you'll begin to be lighted from within and able to give that light to the rest of the world in words, in spirit, in love.

Alice Walker knew the power of letters to promote growth when she wrote *The Color Purple*. The main character, Celie, writes to God because, at fourteen and afraid of more abuse, she fears telling anyone else. The whole book is composed of letters, most of them Celie's. In the first two-thirds of the book, Celie continues to write to God because her sister, Nettie, is apparently dead. But when Celie discovers the truth about her own and her family's mistreatment, she decides that God must be asleep, so she writes only to Nettie until the end of the book. Then she is reunited with her sister, her own missing children, and her dear friend and mentor, Shug. The last letter sums up her awareness and growth as she addresses God, the universe, and all the people in it.

Celie now sees God's presence in all creation. If you write letters, you might too.

Chapter Five

STORIES

Imagination is more important than knowledge.
ALBERT EINSTEIN

If journals and letters develop your voice, stories in your own voice develop your vision. Remember reading or hearing a story and thinking, "I'd like to do that" or "That sounds like my family"? When you followed the story, you found a direction or understood a pattern that opened doors or escape hatches.

Stories help people see their choices. That's why recovery programs such as Alcoholics Anonymous build meetings around real experiences. Telling their stories helps people continue to practice the program (or "walk the talk," in recovery terms), while hearing them reminds listeners to practice too.

Stories also map inner geography. Can you remember your favorite childhood stories? They tell something about how you once saw the world and yourself. One of my favorites was "The Ugly Duckling." I loved the way that ugly (read "different") creature turned into a beautiful, though still different, one. The story shows how I felt at an early stage and explains my lifelong sympathy with people who don't fit. Fortunately, I also had other favorite stories, such as "The Little Engine That Could."

Recalling these childhood stories retrieves bits of my past and fits them into my present. It also helps me understand my assumptions and expectations. What is *your* story-history? Why not recover those tales?

Stories have roots in our most primal selves. They help us make sense of our feelings, especially those we perceive as negative or threatening. They develop into personal and cultural myths and traditions to explain "What happened?" and "Why?"

By addressing those fundamental and sometimes frightening questions, stories make us feel safe. When I felt left out of things years ago, I learned through that duckling that I could eventually join in. So "Once upon a time," still makes me curl up inside like a five-year-old.

Stories are fun, even when they're not funny. We don't mind being frightened because we know it's "just pretend." If a terrifying story is factual, we still take a kind of survivor's satisfaction in knowing that what happened, happened then; we're safe in the light of now. Our larger world may be threatening, as CNN tells us around the clock, but that's "only" television (where both real and unreal take commercial breaks).

Troubling tales also offer outlets for our feelings. The ancient Greeks knew the healing power of scary stories and built their tragedies to show those who, allowing their flaws to dominate them, helped destroy themselves. Watching them, audiences released feelings and enjoyed the relief.

Whether entertaining or sobering, stories draw us in and draw us out of ourselves. And that's just through reading or hearing them. Writing them does even more.

"BUT," you protest, "I'm not creative, so I can't write stories."

Can you write in a journal? Can you write a letter? Then you can write a story, because that's what you've been doing. You just have a restrictive notion of what creativity is and of who is creative. You might like to think about where you got that notion.

The most probable place is school. Did your school have a separate class called Creative Writing? Who took it? Why didn't you? Were you intimidated by people who seemed more sure of themselves than you? Remember that confidence doesn't equal creativity.

What responses did you get to the writing you were required to do? Did your papers look as if your teacher (who was genuinely trying to help) had bled all over them? Did you get comments like "tedious" or "trite," or did you find only negative criticisms without any response to what was alive and strong? Remember that if John Milton were alive today, his teacher would write "misspelled" every time he wrote "heighth," though in the seventeenth century this spelling was correct.

To help yourself recover from criticism-induced creative coma, you need to look at your own credentials. As a start, consider:

- Did you ever explore the woods to find a new trail?
- Did you ever look for shapes in the clouds?
- Did you ever name an animal (or bike or car)? Adam did too.
- Did you ever have an imaginary friend?

- Did you ever make up a story to cover being late? (One of my students explained a late paper with "It's in my other car.")
- Did you ever stage a play (or make costumes or props)?
- Did you ever turn the sofa into an office, cave, or outpost?

What's your "score"? Even if you did only one of these things (or anything else that required or allowed you to adapt, invent, or construct), you *are* creative. Creativity comes from imagination, which is not an option to be earned. It's standard equipment in every human.

What does creativity have to do with prayer? It's a kind of life, for Adam or for you. God can't help being creative. When you use your gifts, you're creative too and are truly God's image. Letting your originality out to play increases your sharing of God's divine fire.

It's time to fan that spark by trying stories. Give yourself this chance to give your *self* a chance. You can do it because you've been doing it all along. Remember that duckling and dive in.

THE SHORT AND THE LONG OF IT

You know that stories can take any form and be any length you want. In fact, there are so few rules for making stories that you might feel unable to start. "Ten Steps to Superb Stories" would ease your fears, but prescriptions don't exist. There are, however, ten guidelines that should help.

1. Slow down. This is not an exam to be completed by three p.m. Let your mind laze so it can catch those wisps of detail or feeling.
2. Start small. Take twenty minutes and begin. You don't have to finish today, or even this year. Take the advice that the king in *Alice's Adventures in Wonderland* gave to the White Rabbit: "Begin at the beginning…and go on till you come to the end: then stop." Each day, just start and stop. Eventually, you'll have a story.
3. Tell the truth. This is what "Write about what you know" means. However, you don't have to have seen a ghost to write about it since you've probably been frightened enough by an unexpected event to have experienced terror's skin, heart, and breathing effects.
4. Be reckless. Don't let the critic in you stop you. Let yourself be crazy, silly, outrageous. Don't look up spelling —right now. The urge to do so is only your critic trying to make you work "perfectly." Keep

going by telling yourself that corrections can wait. (For specific ways to silence your inner critic, see Chapter Seven, "Lists.")
5. Trust yourself. Don't worry about "style"; just write. If you write from your true self, you'll have your own style.
6. Read—later. Feed yourself by reading often. But wait until after you write to avoid using others' words or blocking yourself by comparison with a "pro."
7. Keep secrets. Don't talk about what you're writing. Your unconscious doesn't care how your ideas are expressed as long as they find outlets. So if you talk about your story, you're likely to feel you've done it. If you must talk about it, wait till you're under way.
8. Catch butterflies. You'll get ideas while you're doing something else. (That's why refusing to write works.) So treat ideas as the fragile things they are and net them in detailed notes. If you work on a computer, you won't always be near it or have time to use it, so have writing materials wherever you are. I keep paper in the kitchen, in the bedroom, and even on a clipboard in the car so I can catch whatever flies in. I also use removable notes to add ideas to existing ones; different colors indicate different sections.
9. Cut care-fully. After you've "finished" your story, let it rest so you can distance yourself and see what's there. When you reread, don't look only at errors; look at what this story suggests about where you were, who you were when you wrote it, and where you might go. Of course, you'll want to "correct" your mistakes (especially if you want to show your work to someone else), but your goal is to let your writing help you see possibilities.

    When you do edit, treasure your ideas but cut words wherever you can. Watch out for cliches. You're trying to voice your own vision which, like your fingerprint, is unique. Why would you want to use someone else's words?
10. Find guardians. If you decide to show your story to someone else, make sure the person you choose will respect you and your work. Your story is your "child" in the truest sense, so be careful who handles it. When you let someone read your words, you're honoring that person with your trust because you're allowing them a glimpse of your soul. Find a reader who treasures life and growth.

    I once made the mistake of showing a piece I'd written to a person who cared for me but whose approach to the world was to correct it. He took out a pen and was about to mark up my "baby" when I protested that I didn't want him to change it but to read it. (I really wanted him to admire it!) My excitement over having "finished" it and my need for approval led me to a person who, although he had real good will toward me, could only be who he was.

"WHAT SHALL I WRITE?"

If you follow the guidelines above, you'll begin to write your own story, and as you do, you'll write and develop your self. But these *how* suggestions still leave you with the *big* question: *What* shall I write? The short, simple, and hard answer is—"Anything you want to write."

Still, while it's true that anything honestly done will promote your growth, there are certain kinds of writing that can lead you further along your journey—and one of them might even help you get started. Read through the following possibilities, and use one of them or let them nudge you toward your own possibility.

Whatever you write, remember: this is not a test or an exercise. Relax and let the tale tell you what it can—and will.

Good GOOD Guys and Good BAD Guys

Write a fairy tale. Begin with "Once upon a time" or "Once there was..." Tell about people or animals or machines that have a problem to solve.

Set your story in a place you think is exotic. Let the physical conditions of the place contribute to a problem or its solution. If you choose Bali, for example, use the lush vegetation, the flowers, the sunshine, and the water to help your characters or to frustrate them.

Decide who your story is about. How old is he—or is he a she? How did she get here? Was she born into the situation or brought into it? Does she have special skills? Is she here because of them or in spite of them? Is she alone? How does she look and act? Is her problem a "bad" one such as imprisonment or a "good" one such as an inheritance? How does she react? Does she have a plan? If she's timid, can you put her in charge? What actions show that she is?

Who else is there? Why? How do they respond to your character?

If you usually make everything "nice," include some really bad people and make them as evil as you can. If you usually make everything "pretty," make them ugly. Let them betray, sabotage, slander—whatever you find detestable. And use appropriate language for them. There is no "right" vocabulary, so trying to be proper can zap your story. If your character "sweats," don't say "perspire"—unless that word fits.

Once you get started, let the characters guide you, even surprise you. You can't know all that they'll do or say in advance because they aren't there yet. Once, when William Faulkner was asked about a character in *The Sound and the Fury*, he gave an answer that didn't conform with the book. His young woman had been the way the book presented her at that time, he explained, but she had changed since then.

Let your people go. If you do, you'll have an ending that fits. If it's a "happily ever after" ending, fine. But it doesn't have to be.

Angels and Amazements

Write a story that reveals the invisible. This is a special category of fantasy, although the current popularity of angel books suggests that many people see the fantastic as not necessarily fictitious.

If you believe that the invisible enters into the visible world, you can probably recall a real event in which you or someone you know was helped or protected in a way that defies ordinary logic. Think about that event, letting the details, and especially the feeling, surface. You're looking for effects, since the invisible only becomes apparent through its effects on the visible world.

Were you driving a car, crossing a street, walking a golf course? Were you threatened? What happened? What brought it beyond being an "ordinary" experience?

You can start your story from there, perhaps using letters to tell it. Who's writing? Is this person a believer or a skeptic?

You can also use the real event with invented characters (an FBI agent or a nuclear physicist—though physicists surely know the magic of invisible forces). A skilled observer makes an "impartial" eye witness.

What if you're not a believer or no dramatic example has entered your life? Can you still tell a story of the invisible in the ordinary? Could small accidents be more than coincidental? How can you glimpse those hands or feel those wings? Just start living your daily schedule and watch: bulletins from infinity most often come in whispers. Once you're aware of them, you can write them down.

Where Are You Now, Where Are You Going?

The journey is one of the oldest themes in literature and history. The wanderings of Odysseus, the migrations of tribes, the explorations of new frontiers, all have a journey as their root.

But journeys are spiritual as well as physical. In fact, we make a false distinction by separating them, as if mind and body weren't integrated. As modern medicine rediscovers the truth of the mind/body whole, perhaps we'll heal the split as we heal ourselves.

Each of us is on a journey, even if we never leave our birthplace. Some journeys are simply tours of our daily routines. In taking them, however, we also travel toward or away from what Saint Teresa of Avila called the "interior castle." Because we want to be accepted by our families or our culture, we often leave our real home bases and "adjust" and "adapt" to please others. When we do, we become homesick.

The farther we travel away from ourselves, the more unfamiliar our inner geography seems, until we don't know who we really are. Ironically, we "fit in" wonderfully, but we're lost. When we allow ourselves, we look wistfully at our earlier, truer stages. We need to go home.

Have you felt this longing? Telling a story can help bring you back. But to get *there*, you have to know where *here* is. So begin by writing a story about someone like you.

Choose a name you like or would like to have. I once wrote a story about a thirteen-year-old named Kate. I'm not sure of all of the reasons I like this name, but I like its sound and I like Katharine Hepburn's spirit. What name would you use?

Describe your character's ordinary situation, letting your story grow out of it. For example, you might have this person call a doctor's office to make a long-delayed appointment. In making it, he has to answer questions that fill in details like age and the specific medical complaint.

That phone call can reveal other characteristics too. If he reaches for the phone three times before he actually picks it up, he might be afraid of hearing the bad news medical tests can reveal. If he blames his delay on an overcrowded schedule, he might really have too much to do or he might be procrastinating, which shows another side of fear.

If it's fear of bad news, maybe this person has trouble with aging and his own mortality. What other things about him will reveal his race with reality? What about diet and exercise and clothing and hair? Does he work out fanatically or not at all? Does he ever just sit and think?

Have him connect with others (or not) and react to work, errands, and meals. Or just concentrate on that call and its effects. Does he phone someone? Does he snap at the dog?

What would you like this person to be able to do? You can choose it for him—and for yourself. Write about what *is* for him (or anyone you create) and see what can be for yourself.

Who Are These People?

One of the best ways to see all the factors in your life and claim all of yourself, the parts you like and the ones you don't, is to write a script. This should be the easiest kind of writing, since we're always doing it for other people. Have you ever planned someone's lines?

Scripts reveal through interplay (dialogue) or solo speech (monologue), showing us who characters are even if they don't know themselves. Because "novelistic" narration doesn't fill gaps, our understanding—and theirs—depends on speeches. Characters literally speak for themselves.

They can talk for you, too, showing you parts of yourself you might not know about. When you write a script (or any story form), all the characters are elements of yourself. So script writing can help you hear your whole voice and further your prayer dialogue too.

Scripting is fun. Since it focuses directly on who's doing what to whom by concentrating on speeches, it's a storytelling shorthand. It's also fun because it requires you to hear as you write. You ask yourself, "Would she really say it this way?" Sentence fragments, slang, or hyper-correct language all work, so one character might say, "Yup—right now," while another would say, "Yes, I shall certainly see to it without delay." You can put words in other people's mouths without a problem.

You have to have a problem to start, however, or you have no plot. And while "no problem: no story" is true for all storytelling, it's especially true for a script. You have to move quickly to make the difficulty clear or you just have a lot of small talk—which could be your problem!

Begin, then, with a speech that hints at the issue. Remember when you read *Macbeth* in high school? You learned how important the witches' opening lines are. They clue us in: things are stormy, there's a war, and they'll meet Macbeth later. Those lines set the tone for the whole play.

They also show you that you want to begin in the middle, when the situation has already progressed to a decision-making point. You can lead up to that point slowly in other kinds of storytelling, but in script writing you jump right in. Let your characters argue, complain, praise, refuse; as they do, they'll sketch themselves.

If the thought of writing a whole script scares you, try a scene. Try it especially if you have to resolve a dilemma. Let your characters test your options because, as you're writing for them, you're also writing for yourself. When you're finished, you might be surprised by which alternative you make most convincing.

This kind of externalized talking to yourself lets you reflect on what you're really saying. When you recognize that, you choose knowingly.

If you find you enjoy script writing, try a movie with closeups and voice-overs for hidden reactions. In fact, a great exercise is to write a dialogue with the spoken words followed by those the character really wants to say. There might be no better way to develop your true voice.

If You Can Imagine It...

When you write about someone who achieves the impossible, you use your imagination in a particularly purposeful way. So if you've had a secret wish or dream, write a story and start your own fulfillment.

Creating pictures in your mind creates possibilities. Coaches in all sports know how powerful the imagination is and work to develop images as well as routines in their trainees. Athletes, for example, learn to focus on an interior "film" that shows them performing as they wish to. Those who focus best, perform best. If the skills exist, limits disappear.

If you're stuck or afraid or squirming, write about someone stuck like you who goes to New York, lives alone, asks for an interview, speaks up, talks back, auditions for the part, submits the proposal, takes art (computer, speech, dance) classes, climbs a mountain, goes skydiving, or does anything you'd like to try. As you write, picture each detail. If you want to do massage therapy, picture the room, the table, the oils and lotions, the CD player, the disks, the desk. Picture yourself going into the room and working on someone. Picture your movements. Feel your strokes. Writing it out is a safe way to take a step toward freedom.

Be forewarned, however: if you invest yourself in your character you'd better be ready to get moving. Envisioning—really seeing yourself free—helps free you. And free people are the ones who have something to say in the conversation with God called prayer.

Chapter Six

NEWSPAPER PIECES

*I see heaven's glory shine,
and faith shines equal, arming me from fear.*

EMILY BRONTE

While you might not think of newspaper articles as stories in the same way that fairy tales are, you can use their forms imaginatively to increase your vision and understanding. You can also use the techniques of newspaper writing to help you develop compassion and forgiveness. When you learn to see people objectively, your own emotional filters melt away.

Increasingly, professional writers deliberately cross from fact to fiction and back again, blending novelistic and journalistic techniques to give an inside view of characters and events. Examples of fictionalized facts abound in the historical novels of James Michener or in Alex Haley's *Roots*. If you've read any of these tales, you know how you can learn about the past and develop great empathy at the same time.

You don't have to choose a famous person or historical period to benefit from writing "news" pieces, however. Your family and your own exploits furnish abundant material, showing another application of the "write what you know" principle. Just look around you, and you'll learn how to look inside. When you do, you'll see your particular world's history differently.

BIOGRAPHIES

Some people insist that history is really a series of biographies. Certainly, studying the past as a group of interwoven human stories makes the merely academic vibrate with life. To see people instead of facts is to care; to see people as they are is to understand.

So if you want to understand *care*-fully, write a biography. Take any puzzling or frustrating situation and write about at least one of the characters involved as if you didn't know him or her and were merely compiling a piece for publication.

For instance, suppose your parents live in New York City, and despite your urging, they refuse to move from an increasingly troubled neighborhood to a safer location. You've reasoned with them, presented alternatives, offered statistics—all without success. They simply will not move.

You can't force them to move, since they're competent and able to decide for themselves. Legally, even morally, you can't do anything. So write about your parents as they began to develop their attachment to this place, perhaps when they were newlyweds in their first apartment. Describe each room and its furnishings: the kitchen table, the new curtains, the bedroom set bought on an installment plan. Have them talk about hopes for family and future. Hear them reassure their own parents. See them feeling independent and free.

If you mine your memory by letting fragments surface as you write, you may find you know more than you thought you did about those early years before you were born, before responsibility weighed your parents down. You've probably heard stories about how they lived. You might even have seen snapshots from the days when they seemed so adventurous.

If you don't have all the information you need, ask. If you can't ask, invent. This is where your imagination can help you understand. Picture their surroundings by starting with what you know your parents like now and envisioning what they liked then. Be where they were. After putting yourself in their place, you can begin to feel for and with them.

By the time you finish, you might be able to admire their determination, even if you still want them to move. You haven't changed them; you've opened a new perspective in yourself. And your increased understanding might just let them feel free enough to change their minds.

This technique is especially helpful in healing wounds suffered in even the best-willed families. If you're angry toward your mother and can't forgive what she did to or didn't do for you, write about her as she grew up in her own birth family. Picture her clearly: her face and hair, her clothing, her surroundings. Have her talk to *her* mother. How does her mother respond? What postures do they each assume? How does your mother look afterward?

If you can learn to see as a camera does, looking through an impartial lens, you will see and feel in ways you couldn't before. If you begin to envision even those with whom you're furious as toddlers, you'll perceive them differently. You might not be able to change them, but you've changed the situation because you've changed—and freed—yourself.

You can adapt this approach for use with older people, contemporaries, and younger people too. For example, if you seem always to lock horns with one of your children, try writing about yourself from that child's perspective. This could include a view of you as a giant with enormous power and skill, always doing things right and always winning in confrontations. Your description might include the pitch of your voice or certain pet phrases ("Because I said so!").

When you're finished, see if there's a question that emerges from your piece. Suppose you now suspect that your son's routine blowups might come from his perceiving your "advice" as criticism. A statement such as "When I tell you what I would do in your place, how do you feel?" lets him know you really want to understand him and perhaps already do. It also lets you think about how you like criticism.

Writing biographies can open your eyes and your heart. And when you open them, you clear the way for compassion—which means to "suffer with"—and even for forgiveness.

AUTOBIOGRAPHIES

If history is a collection of biographies, it's also a series of autobiographies. But while biographies recall events as acted, autobiographies voice events as felt. Their first-person view precludes the objectivity that biographies claim. However, they do offer a special kind of "truth."

You can use this ancient form to see yourself with clarity and compassion. If you write your story, you help put the pieces in order as if you were arranging an album. You know how it helps you to talk about a particular event with a friend. Imagine how helpful putting it all down can be.

For example, you can wonder about a seemingly meaningless detail like your birthplace. Thomas Merton considered the fact that he was born in Prades, France, significant enough to meditate upon throughout his adulthood. What is your birthplace? Can you see symmetry between it and your life? (Mine is Philadelphia. Does my habit of questioning rules have anything to do with that?)

What about your position in the family? What were your advantages—and disadvantages? Can you see how your position shaped you? (I'm the third of eight, so I learned to find my own way early.)

As you examine each stage of your journey, be open not only to details like the schools you attended but also to the special bits that make you who you are. Did you have a favorite tree? What kind was it?

What were your favorite foods when you were nine? What colors did you like? Did you pick blackberries or collect rocks? Did you go to camp? Did you have a crush on a classmate? Did you skip classes?

Did you have a favorite sweater in high school? Did you go to a prom and like it or suffer through it? Did you "accidentally" meet anyone who changed your way of thinking about things?

Your autobiography is a big project but it shouldn't be too daunting since you have all the material inside you. In fact, writing your story will help you reclaim countless "lost" pieces of yourself. You have the rest of your life to tell it, and only you can tell it your way.

You *can* tell someone else's story, though, even if you're not Gertrude Stein, who wrote *The Autobiography of Alice B. Toklas*. In fact, writing someone else's story from that person's "I" could be your most powerful way of becoming compassionate. The Native American injunction about walking in another's moccasins requires the same empathy.

If you want to understand someone, then, especially a someone who's troublesome to you, write her autobiography. Emphasize childhood and adolescence, since these are the sources of your subject's present self. If you don't have all the facts you need and can't get them, imagine key situations and put the person in them. Let her tell her tale: at three, eleven, thirteen, seventeen. You're writing a kind of fiction, anyway, so use your sensitivities and senses to get a whole picture.

This exercise is a good accompaniment to letters to and from someone in your past whom you no longer can "speak" with in ordinary ways. It's a way of listening to voices in your life and therefore in yourself.

PRESS RELEASES

Another journalistic model you can use to help clarify your vision is the press release. We're flooded with press releases every day and distrust them because we sense they're produced by publicists to promote a particular—and not particularly truthful—point of view.

But suppose you want a brief, alternative, outside view of a situation in which you are emotionally involved. You want to use your "camera eye" to take a snapshot that allows you to distance yourself from the emotional tangle.

Try untangling your feelings by writing a few sentences about what troubles you. Use the Journalism 101 formula, as if this were all the information you or anyone else had. Who, what, where, when, and why did so-and-so choose as she did?

Remember the famous television detective who insisted on "just the facts, ma'am"? By doing your own "write byte," you lay out what an uninvolved person knows. But you also challenge your own perspective. Is it possible that what upsets (angers, frustrates, distracts) you so could be seen in an entirely different way by others? Is the stress in the *situation* or in *you*?

You can use the same shorthand formula to look at yourself. Instead of the "I" that you've used in journals and letters, give your name as you would anyone else's. This might feel strange, but try it.

Writing just the facts not only helps you think about your own predicament, it also helps you get it "out there" where you can look at it. You might have to look hours or days later, but at least you can shift your gaze and glimpse the possibility that the difficulty exists because you've identified with your problem. You've let it take you over, so it's all you can focus on.

Your little blurb doesn't blame you; it just says what is. It also shows you that there's more to you than this situation, overwhelming as it feels. It's one—and only one—part of your journey. When you see that, you might still face a problem, but you're not knotted into immobility.

I can't emphasize enough that this exercise isn't about blaming; it's about distinguishing between *what is* and *how you feel* about it. It allows you to pick up clues that could lead you out of the emotional labyrinth. If you find those threads, you're on your way to freedom.

You can also use this exercise to try out a decision you're debating. Write different versions and let them rest. When you reread them, ask yourself if someone else would see any other choices. You could find you have more options than you realized. You might even learn to like choosing!

OBITUARIES

A fourth journalistic model is the obituary, that usually sketchy outline of a life that ended. While obituaries aren't fun to think about (despite their being called the "Irish funnies"), they are realities that make us consider where we've been and where we want to head.

If you want to meditate on your priorities, write your own obituary. In two or three paragraphs, include your full name, age, place of death, birthplace, schooling, job history, affiliations with church and social groups, and survivors.

Why would you even think about doing such a sobering, if not morbid, thing? For one thing, it gets your attention fast: this is life, it's not a dress rehearsal.

Also, it makes choices simpler because it places them in perspective. Daily difficulties shrink to their appropriate size in this written version of "If you only had one day to live, what would you do?" The long view examines whether everything deserves the same effort. You can see what matters and be freed of enslavement to the rest.

You might have experienced a version of this freedom while waiting for the results of a troubling medical examination. Somehow, other concerns seemed less important, if not trivial. You were preoccupied with the present and what it held or threatened.

You also valued other people more during this crisis. If you didn't want to talk, you took comfort in their willingness to be with you. You might even have made resolutions about how you were going to order your future. Was there someone you wanted to bring back into your life? Was there anything you wanted to say that you'd been putting off? Crises—real or imaginary—help you find the courage to connect.

Writing your final story contributes to life, not death, since it makes the time you have more precious. You remember how wonderful, terrible, and rich your time is and end by being grateful you're alive.

Writing your own obituary also makes you more sensitive to those who are facing imminent death. Terminally ill patients often feel isolated because even loving friends and relatives avoid them or don't let them talk explicitly about their final stages. Your open-eyed look at your own mortality can make you more comfortable with someone's actual dying. You enrich your life by living more intensely, and you enrich the life of the other person too.

You spend many hours and days trying to direct your life, to make it rewarding. If you risk spending a few minutes on considering its last steps, you'll make the journey itself immeasurably more fruitful. You'll also find your examination overflowing naturally into ever more honest dialogue with God.

Chapter Seven

LISTS

A person's life should be as fresh as a river. It should be the same channel but a new water every instant.

HENRY DAVID THOREAU

One of the simplest and most ordinary ways of discovering what wants or needs voicing in you is to make lists. If you are puzzled about a new possibility—or trying to find a new possibility—lists help you let your inner wisdom surface. They also show you just how inventive, playful, and even funny your deepest self is.

Since you've made lists all your life, you already know how list-writing coaxes you toward consciousness. Even when you forget the list, you remember your objectives better than if you hadn't made one.

Lists work because they help you hold ideas twice: once when you think of them and a second time when you write them. Those who study memory know that the more ways you impress anything on your conscious mind, the better your chances of "learning" it. You learn through your senses, so the more sensory your process, the more permanent your gain.

Lists also work because they allow you to order and reorder their contents. You set priorities by your arrangement. Of course, the items you choose to include show your priorities as well.

Some lists work better than others, however. Did you ever make a self-improvement list, perhaps at New Year's, and find you weren't observing it by January 12? You have a lot of company.

List-making as self-wrenching doesn't work. One reason is that the resistance it sets up tires us, usually sooner rather than later. A more fundamental reason is that we were never meant to make life a do-it-yourself-until-you're-perfect project. Our journeys are about claiming all that's in us, not about amputating or killing parts of ourselves.

The very elements we don't like to face could be the ones that show us what we need to notice. The more we try to eradicate them, the more insistently they surface.

The lists you use for developing your voice—and therefore your prayer—aren't prescriptions for self-inflicted surgery, much less spiritual implants. Instead, these verbal cardiograms will help you see your present state and give hints about where you might head and how to get there. They give quick sketches of your soul.

Of course, these are not your daily go-to-the-supermarket lists, although they can start in the same way. They are also not the dreaded "outlines" you wrote in school, with all the structure and stricture those numbers and letters suggest.

Instead, these are lists that help you associate freely, producing a written, benign kind of "brainstorming." Some people use special names for them, such as "clustering" or "mind mapping," but they're still lists. You don't need anything special to let them help you. However, you do need a few simple materials.

- *Paper.* Use blank paper. Lines suggest a "right" direction, and there is no predetermined pattern. Sheets should be large, at least eight and one-half by eleven inches, since you'll want to spread out. However, once when I was on a plane and had nothing else, I used a four-by-five-inch notepad and caught lots of ideas with that. *Any* paper will do. Try recycling the backs of old letters and photocopies.
- *Pen or pencil.* Use whatever feels most flowing. Fiber-tip pens give some people a sense of speed. Try as many instruments as you can.
- *Color.* Have colored pens or crayons ready to use for organizing items once you've completed the list. Choose distinctly contrasting colors. For example, if you use blue ballpoint to list, don't select a blue crayon. Contrast will help, as you'll soon see.

If you're "hooked" on your word processor and want to use it, you can, but you'll miss the free movement that pen or pencil on paper gives. You might find that because your machine works in a linear way, your thinking also tends to remain linear when you use a word processor. So for best results, list by hand.

The only other thing you will need is a few undisturbed minutes. Everything else is in you; you only need to let it out. When you do, you'll hear yourself better and have more voice for prayer.

SHAPE ISN'T EVERYTHING

In our shape-obsessed culture, you'll find refuge from the "right" look by taking a look at yourself with a list. This is one place where you can honor your spirit's urge to *be messy*. In fact, trying to be orderly can work against you in listing, so prepare for the written equivalent of finger painting and slide all over your project.

To help your consciousness get the message that the usual rules don't apply, begin in the middle of the page instead of at the top, left-hand side. Then try the following steps.

- *Write one word.* Choose one that states your question or subject. You can also use a phrase or proverb, especially if it feels like your motto for the moment.
- *Circle your subject.* This is your core and everything will emerge from it. You circle it because you're reminding (re-minding) yourself where you are—at your "core" self.
- *Tune in now.* Write the first word that comes to mind. Place it anywhere on the page and circle it. Write the next word, then the next, then the next. Circle them as you go. Write as many as you can, letting them form any kind of pattern. Don't even think about shape; just let it happen.

My words have sprayed, spiraled, and whipped on the page. I don't remember ever having made a straight line for more than an inch or two.

After you practice this kind of listing and become comfortable with it, you can try using words without circles. But if you find you get stuck often, keep circling and connecting your circles with lines or arrows. This will keep your hand moving and help get your mind moving again.

ONE THING LEADS TO ANOTHER

Your objective as you move across the page is to capture as many ideas and images as possible. You don't have to work at them. In fact, the less directive you are, the more you'll find fragments you had "lost" to time, stress, and activity. Consider yourself on automatic and just let the words flow onto the paper through your hand. Continue writing this way.

- *Wonder and wander.* Follow your ideas as you would a new path that you're sure will lead to excitement and satisfaction. Write foolishness, song titles, lines of poems, rhyming words, advertising slogans, even nonsense sounds.
- *Continue to write.* Go as far as you can with your shape. If you run dry, retrace your circles or reconnect them. You can also return to your center to take a new direction, or you can spin off one of the circles on your "spokes" or "plumes."
- *Stop on command.* Follow your inner pilot until you feel pulled in a certain direction or until you sense that you know what you need to know or want to say. This may be very clear and explicit—such as when you have a sudden insight—or it may happen gradually. But if you keep wandering and writing, it *will* happen.

FASTER THAN A SPEEDING CRITIC

When you're trying to list this way for the first time, you might be tempted to make your lines just *so* or to ignore certain words. This is your left brain trying to be helpful. But you have to outrun it if you're going to let your own genie (meaning *genius*) out. So write as fast as you can to beat your brain out of criticism.

It's important to suspend judgment. Remember, no one will rate your list, not even on its being first in foolishness. In fact, no one will see it (unless you choose to show it). Tell your interior critic there will be a job to do soon, but for now, you and your hand are just out to play.

If you're working in a group, don't worry if you're not writing as much as the person next to you. The size of your list will vary with your subject.

After you've written all you think you can, try for more. More here means more outrageous, fanciful, or silly rather than merely more in quantity. Capture all you can, but know that different facets of the same fragment might be more helpful than a consciously developed new chain of images.

MAKING CONNECTIONS

Once you've followed your instincts and your images as far as you need to and have an inkling of what you want to know or explore, write a phrase or a sentence that summarizes your insight. Just write what feels true, even if it seems strange or unlikely. You're trying to connect with your deepest self and draw on that inner wisdom, so expect the unexpected.

Write your summary even if it seems preposterous—a "Who, me?" experience. Maybe you're being drawn to a new way to be. Honor that and reinforce it.

Reread your summary, adding whatever seems necessary for clarity. Since you won't be able to replicate this exact series of moments, you want to be able to understand and integrate what you've found.

Now reread your list. Use one of the colors you selected to mark related ideas and images. You might use green rectangles for one set, red triangles for another, and purple diamonds for a third. You could be surprised to find that phrases and even whole sentences have "written themselves." Outline those in color too.

Expect elements that don't fit, that even seem to mean the opposite of the words they follow. These contrasts are natural and sound. If you think "light," for example, you can only imagine it if you have some concept of "dark." Opposites are parts of wholes, and your inner self is a whole, even if you don't see all its sides. Listing will help you see them.

When you find these contrasts, value them. William Blake wrote, "Without contraries there is no progression." You need opposites to progress, whether you're driving by correcting the steering from side to side or traveling metaphorically on your life's journey. So let opposites speak to you and guide you to a new or clearer direction.

The important final step is to save your list by adding it to your journal or by filing it in a folder. Date this page so you'll be able to place it later as you follow your journey.

File your list in your soul too. Just as you wrote with wonder, admire the wonder and richness of your spirit. Rejoice in the ingenious, unique creation you are. You have all you need to dialogue with God, so set it—and yourself—free.

TAKING DIRECTIONS

Use your new insight to open up your prayer. Whether you turn to your journal, write a letter, or invent a story, being open means being receptive, empty, and willing. It means leaving holes in defenses, instead of plugging them up in an effort to keep things as they are. Openness takes courage.

And you have courage; you just demonstrated it by letting yourself loose in your list. In fact, picking up this book shows that you're genuinely courageous.

So open the ears of your heart and listen to what your spirit is whispering. Your spirit takes flight in the Spirit that makes everything new. It will help you turn holes into holiness.

Take Your Cue

Let your newly formed insight direct you as a good movie director does: by nurturing, coaxing, inviting what's inside to become apparent. For example, when I was jobless several years ago, I wrote a list that centered on fear. At first, I used a lot of dark and scary words and images, but these became mixed with ghost stories and haunted houses. Then my list shifted to children's games. No matter which swirl I wrote, I reached light and play.

When I finished, I felt better because I sensed I was protected. My inner self told me I was safe, and I was grateful. My prayer sprang out like the playful seal with the ball on its nose on my list.

My awareness of safety also urged me to play in my grown-up life as I had on paper. So I used the same kind of listing to dream up projects I would relish. Those projects not only found me jobs, they also helped me feed my spirit by sharing work I love.

Your inner self can direct you too. Start with the awareness you reach through your list. Let it coax you to be who you were born to be.

Take Your Mark

You might know that television performers have to stand in places that are marked on the floor. Production crews need certain distances so that cameras can get close-ups, distance shots, and panoramic views.

You can use this model to let your lists direct you. When you center yourself as you start your writing, you take (and make) your mark. By allowing yourself to receive the predictable and unpredictable bits that surface, you also allow yourself to receive and focus on yourself. That list of fragments is a close-up of your spirit at a particular moment: a real verbal "head shot" that's a heart shot too.

But your list gives you a distance shot as well, since it lets you stand back, rest, and return to it to see what general outlines are there. When you begin to find related images and ideas, you also see the skeleton of a situation or question and spot a theme you might be able to take further.

When you take the distant view of your spirit-search, you also start to sense how this stage fits into or builds upon your life's journey to this point. With patience and practice, you recognize that even the most pressing issues are only parts of your "soulscape's" panorama and that your situation is, in turn, part of the larger community of spirits. You also open yourself to more coaching and coaxing because you sense you have a part here that no one else can play.

No one else can, just as no one else can produce a verbal picture exactly like yours. So take your mark by starting at your center and spinning—yourself.

Take Off

If you've ever been on a plane, you'll remember the last seconds before take off, when the plane gathers speed but creaks and groans with resistance because of gravity's pull. There's a moment when gravity and speed struggle to dominate each other, and after that seemingly eternal but very brief tussle, the plane breaks loose and starts to climb.

Our spirits fight against flight just as that plane does. We groan and shudder and complain when we try to free ourselves from the daily pressures and pulls of our lives. Staying in the same place is easier than getting ourselves moving.

Listing can help us take off. As our hands move faster and faster across the paper, we gather momentum and invite the lift that will help us soar. We leave creeping behind and fling ourselves toward a path we need to take.

When you list and listen to yourself, you break free.

Chapter Eight

FILL IN THE BLANKS

I desire no future that will break the ties of the past.
GEORGE ELIOT

Do you remember taking tests that asked you to complete a statement? Usually you had to supply facts by filling in words. When you did, you were finished.

You might have liked those exercises because you didn't have to write much to succeed. They even made studying easier since you looked for answers instead of the connections that essays demanded.

Those fill-ins can be useful as measures of fact retention (even if that retention is short-term). But they can also give a limited impression of learning as merely giving the "right" answer. Learning is a thoughtful process. Still, there is a way to use fill-ins to fill in your own story and expand your awareness. If the questions are open-ended, they promote real understanding and support growth.

In addition, if you're feeling flat and unable to come up with a single thing to write, fill-ins can get you started. You can use them as themes for a day, a week, or as long as you find them fruitful and, even better, fun.

So try to complete some of the statements below. When you do, remember:

Exceed the "limit." There is no right content or length for your answer, but you'll gain more by writing beyond the starter sentence than you will by filling it in and stopping. You want to avoid the written equivalent of the conversation stopper. You're trying to encourage a dialogue with your inner self and with God.

Fill all the blanks with details. If "the devil's in the details," as computer people say, God is in them even more. So when a starter draws on your memory, use your powerful imagination to put yourself back there, where and when the event you're focusing on occurred. Use all your senses and see, hear, taste, touch, and smell the situation. Include it all, even if you don't have time at one sitting. The more real you make it, the more whole it can make you.

Love your enemies. Some of these starters will be easier for you to develop than others, so you'll have no trouble writing about them. But a few might make you react strongly, even negatively. If they do, consider writing about them anyway. You might find just the clue you want or uncover just the memory you need to make sense of why you are where you are right now.

We don't learn much that's new from our friends because we already know what they're like; that's why they're our friends. Maybe we have to expand the notion of "friend" to include those people and things that hold up a mirror in front of us so we can see *all* of who we are.

You have nothing to fear from your feelings even if you have painful memories. If you use all you have, you'll grow. Margaret Walker once said that if she wrote long enough, she'd write herself sane. You can write yourself whole.

Remember, your purpose is to find your voice so you can pray in it. That means your full voice, with all its tones and shadings. Your laughing, crying, moaning, giggling, sassy, soft, sharp, hard, angry, teasing, soothing, peaceful voice is your full voice. Fill in the parts you're muffling by filling in your blanks.

IN TWENTY-FIVE WORDS OR MORE

Use any or all of the following to start your search. When you're "finished," reread. Then rest—and notice how you feel and what you want to say.

- I'm most myself when…
- My ideal day would be…
- I'm most like my father in…
- I'd like to learn…
- If I could tell my three-year-old self one thing, it would be…
- I'm least myself when…
- If I had no responsibilities, I would…
- People usually describe me as…

- At age eleven:
    - *my secret place was...*
    - *I loved to eat...*
    - *my favorite rainy-day activity was...*
    - *my favorite person was...*
- If I could afford it, I'd...
- I wonder why...
- I wish I could tell just one person...
- I'm most like my mother in...
- I'm afraid...
- If my life were a color, it would be...
- If I could write my own eulogy, I would say...
- The best things about me are...
- One thing I can do to be more myself is...
- If my life were a dance, it would be...

GETTING THE PICTURE

Another way of filling in the blanks is to use old pictures. If you're lucky enough to have snapshots of your earlier years, let one of them help you start writing about a situation in your past or let a series of photographs prompt you to tell about progressive stages.

Old pictures also lead you to rewrite an emotion-torn time, so that instead of continuing to fight or struggle, you accept what was and what is. When you accept, you move toward healing and forgiveness.

You can use old pictures to refocus a rift between yourself and a parent, for instance. If you had a distant or difficult relationship, looking at each of you—or if you're lucky, both of you together—lets you begin to gaze with the "soft eyes" that take everything in but don't narrow in judgment. So raid the family album or picture box and dig out a prize.

If you're a parent, you can also use pictures to relive a family experience and revise (which means to re-see) it. You might discover that you want to reinforce and confirm one of your children or your spouse. You can also redirect a relationship, even if what you end up doing is deciding to do nothing: to give up your previous attempts to fix and control and make things better. You might be amazed at the tenderness you feel for someone who often "pushes your hot button."

So, whether you're dealing with your birth family, your current family, or someone totally unrelated, find a picture that captures what you want to explore, and begin.

Go Through the Lens

Select a photograph that invites you, either because of its subject or because of the feeling it arouses in you. Don't try to explain the feeling—at least not yet; just feel it. And don't write yet. Let the picture rest in front of you as you rest your gaze on it. Enter the scene as if you were walking through the lens.

Experience the moment with all your senses. If it's a wintry outdoor scene, feel the chilling wind and the texture of your coat; hear the frost crunch under your feet and the click of the shutter; smell your mother's perfume. Can you hear voices? Are they angry? Jubilant? Notice exactly what is happening in front of the camera.

If you're not in the picture, enter it as much as you can. For example, I have a fragile photograph of my grandmother and great aunt taken when they were in their early twenties, before they married. It makes me feel contented and connected to feel the sun on their arms through long, white sleeves and the shade on their faces under those big hats. I can smell the hay and hear the crickets and taste the grape juice they had on that summer day. I never knew them when they were so carefree, and I'm grateful for their willingness to embrace life.

Give It Voice

Ask the question(s) you couldn't ask then. In the example I just gave, since my great aunt has her hands on her hips, I imagine she's saying, "Now, really!" as she often did. I can ask her why she's standing like that and what she really said. Was she flirting? I like to think she was—with my great uncle. Was she teasing? She teased a lot, and since it sometimes bothered me as a child, it helps me to see this as part of her, not as something specially aimed at me.

If you're alone in the picture, question yourself; if you're accompanied, write to the other person. Remember that your goal is understanding, not blaming, so ask for information without accusing.

For instance, if that wintry scene shows you and your mother, who looks pretty frosty herself, you might write, "Mom, were you angry with me? Is that why you didn't put your arm around me?"

Then write the answer—or part of it. Keep the dialogue going until you hear what you need to know. This "scripting" starts with a reality, or appears to. But a photo can only record what a lens can see; there's often much more going on.

If you can't write a dialogue right now, try writing a brief note about how you feel.

Act It Out

After you write your dialogue or note, wait quietly but expectantly, as if you were waiting to hear a secret. You are. You're holding yourself open so you can be receptive, like a tuned-in stereo system. You want to honor your feeling and your awareness with an action.

Suppose that you're gazing at a picture of yourself at the age of three and you're sad because you sense how vulnerable you were. Write your script or note to that child. Then be alert for what you want to do next. Do you want to blow bubbles or swing as high as you can? Do you want to hug? Do you want to hold out your hand in invitation? Do something physical, however small, that honors your present feelings and your past. You don't have to do it publicly as long as you *do* it.

Next consider how you can incorporate the past in the picture into your current life. If you feel more understanding of someone, can you write a letter and send it? If you're conscious of a shift to a new stage, can you plant a flower? If you recognize that you've been too busy with the grown-up world, can you take a day off and walk barefoot on the beach? If you're feeling safer and freer, can you phone a family member?

Whatever you do, do something that takes your awareness into your routine. Consider whether you want to build this practice into your life. If you do, you'll honor your past as you honor yourself and your growth. Just like that three-year-old, you need to know your feelings count, and you need to value them enough to act on them.

Scripture urges us to choose life. When you reclaim your past with the help of pictures, you choose—and celebrate—life. Your words and actions tell your deepest self that you treasure all of who you are. And when you value yourself, you praise God with your own unique voice.

APPENDIX

TEN TIPS FOR PRAYING IN YOUR OWN VOICE

1. Pray at any time and in any place, using any posture, any words, and any tone. You can *be* the prayer as well as the pray-er.
2. Pray by conversing with God. Sometimes you'll be active, sometimes receptive, and sometimes both.
3. Write to help yourself think, discern, grow. Write to pray.
4. Make time work for you by taming it with a timer.
5. Move your hand to move your brain.
6. Find your voice by journaling. Materials matter less than being open, honest, faithful, and respectful—of yourself.
7. Refine your voice with letters. Write them to yourself, to others, to God.
8. Enlarge your vision with stories. Use techniques from fiction (such as fairy tales and scripts) or nonfiction (such as biographies and obituaries) to see *and* understand.
9. Let your real self out to play—and pray—by writing lists.
10. Fill in your blanks by using starters and pictures.

FOR RETREAT DIRECTORS

Have you ever wondered if retreatants take anything away from conferences? Would you like them to take what they hear deeper into their own spirits? This book can help.

It shows you how to use writing to recall, retain, and integrate your suggestions with the retreatants' own insights. It supports and reinforces what you do by inviting reflection and interweaving it with daily life. It encourages discernment and growth.

But it has one drawback: it demands *your* personal involvement. You know that authenticity grows out of experience. So if you want to encourage those in your care to write toward wholeness, you have to try it yourself. The following guidelines will help:

Do it yourself. Inventory your own writing habits and any fears you may have. Since fear blocks writing, if you recognize your own fear, you can connect with others as they try these very personal forms. Common ground helps you help others.

As you read this book, sample its possibilities. When you find one that fits, practice it long enough to be comfortable with it: a few weeks of brief journal entries, for example, will show you how this model works and will carry over to your routine.

Choose your tools. Adopt a form (or two) that suits your style and plan; then adapt it to your needs. Journals and letters are easiest for most beginners, since other types can be frightening or may require materials (such as pictures) you might not have at hand. On the other hand, those who are advanced in their spiritual journeys might already be keeping journals or writing letters, so stories could help them more.

Depending on your theme or goal, you might want to use some of the fill-in-the-blank exercises as starters. You can also choose a word, phrase, or passage to aid spiritual movement. Just remember that whatever you use, it has to connect with life experience—yours and your group's. People have to feel "This is about me."

Prepare your group. If you want to integrate writing fully, let people know before you begin. You can do this in your brochure. If you think that might prove too daunting, you can introduce it in the opening conference. If *you're* sold on journaling, you won't need to say much because you'll know and so will your group through your brief (please!) description. That's why you have to try these forms yourself.

So as you begin
- tell people they'll write during the retreat
- assure them they won't have to share
- give specific (non-)directions: no required length, no special words, no prescribed structure
- give a starter (After a conference, for example, ask participants to write about one word or idea that struck them.)

Make it possible. You probably schedule open time in all your retreats. If you don't, arrange some now. People need to gather wool and find their own rhythms, especially when they write.

You also need to provide

- paper or notebooks
- pens or pencils
- colors (A few bright crayons will be fine.)

If you want people to use pictures, ask them to bring some. You can also clip photos that complement your theme from magazines and let people choose.

Try to write yourself as you let the Spirit lead you and your group. Not only will you model the behavior you want to encourage, you will also hear the constantly deepening whispers in your own heart. You'll glimpse new possibilities for your work and life.

I pray you find joy in discovery.

FOR FURTHER READING

Journals

If you want to read examples of others' searches, try one of these.

Hillesum, Etty. *An Interrupted Life: The Diaries of Etty Hillesum, 1941-1943.* New York: Washington Square Press, 1985. A young Jewish woman who died in a Nazi concentration camp kept this journal from 1941 to 1943. It shows how, as her voice developed, her spirituality changed and deepened, bringing her from apathy toward God and spirit, to an awareness of God's presence, to a commitment to bringing life despite her imprisonment. You will live and feel with Etty.

Lewis, C.S. *A Grief Observed.* New York: Bantam Books, 1983. Lewis wrote this journal to help himself deal with his doubts about God and his anger, fear, and grief after the death of his wife, Joy Davidman. His honest writing not only helped him find peace but also created one of the most consoling books about loss ever written. Read it once a year.

Merton, Thomas. *The Sign of Jonas.* New York: Harcourt Brace, 1979. Although all of Merton's journals deserve attention, this one, which covers about five years of his early life at Gethsemani, shows his approaches to (and often wrestling matches with) God and his struggles to find true solitude. It is also a model of journaling as a help toward growth. It shows Merton's humanity (witty, irreverent, imperfect, *and* reverent, devoted, and obedient) as well as his deep spiritual hunger. It promotes and encourages prayer.

Writing

These will enlighten and encourage you if you want to do more writing.

Brande, Dorothea. *Becoming a Writer.* Los Angeles: Tarcher, 1981. This helps cultivate the attitudes, habits, and temperament of writers. Brande discusses the unconscious/conscious complementarity and gives practical, concrete advice for the beginner or anyone who wants to begin again. Because it focuses on the heart as well as the mind, this one deserves shelf space.

Metzger, Deena. *Writing for Your Life: Discovering the Story of Your Life's Journey.* San Francisco: Harper SF, 1992. If you want to explore your creativity, this books offers almost limitless possibilities. Even if you only sample it, it helps you unlock your own rich store of ideas as you develop stories and promote healing. It makes you reach for your pen.

Ueland, Brenda. *If You Want to Write: A Book About Art, Independence and Spirit.* Saint Paul, MN: Graywolf Press, 1987. If you have room or time for only one book on writing (and living with vitality), this is the one. It's not only about writing, it's about anything you love and invest yourself in and relish. Take this one with you to that desert island. It's my favorite!